be retur

DNA & GENETIC ENGINEERING

Robert Snedden

Series Editor
Andrew Solway

Heinemann
LIBRARY

First published in Great Britain by Heinemann Library, Halley Court, Jordan Hill, Oxford OX2 8EJ, a division of Reed Educational and Professional Publishing Ltd. Heinemann is a registered trademark of Reed Educational & Professional Publishing Ltd.

OXFORD MELBOURNE AUCKLAND JOHANNESBURG BLANTYRE GABORONE IBADAN PORTSMOUTH NH (USA) CHICAGO

Designed by Paul Davies and Associates
Illustrations by Wooden Ark
Originated by Ambassador Litho Ltd.
Printed by Wing King Tong in Hong Kong.

06 05 04 03 02
10 9 8 7 6 5 4 3 2 1
ISBN 0 431 14711 6

British Library Cataloguing in Publication Data

Snedden, Robert
   DNA & genetic engineering. – (Cells and life)
   1.DNA – Juvenile literature 2.Genetic engineering – Juvenile literature
   I.Title
   572.8'6

Acknowledgements

The Publishers would like to thank the following for permission to reproduce photographs:
Corbis:J L Amos pg 10, /U Walz pg 28; FPG/ J Cummins pg 4; PA Photos: pg 35; Powerstock Photo Library: pg 38; Science Photo Library: M Baret (Rapho) pg 31, /J Berger, Max Planck Institute, pgs 14 and 16, /Biology Media pg 22, /BSIP, LA/FILIN Herrera pg 42, /J Burgess pg 27, /M Fermariello pg 23, /S Fraser pg 40, /M Iwafuji pg 32, /J King-Holmes pg 21, /A Leonard pg 37, /M Lewis, University of Pennsylvania Medical Center, pg 11, /K Lounatmaa pg 12, /P Menzel pg 25, /H Morgan pg 13, /S Moulds pg 29(t), /G Murti pgs 5, 15 and18, /Y Nikas pg 36, /Omikron pg 9, /D Parker pgs 20, 41 and 43, /M Read pg 26, /S Stammers pg 24, /G Tompkinson pg 39, /J C Revy pgs 33 and 34, /M Whitaker pg 30, /E Young (Agstock) pg 29(b).

Cover photo reproduced with permission of Science Photo Library/P M Motta and S Makabe.

Our thanks to Richard Fosbery for his comments in the preparation of this book, and also to Alexandra Clayton.

Contents

*Words in bold, **like this,** are in the Glossary.*

1 Nature's way

People have very different views about genetic engineering. Genetically modified (GM) crops such as soy beans that are resistant to insecticides are now widely grown for food, but many people think that eating such foods is a risk. The first artificially **cloned** animal, Dolly the sheep, was born in 1997, and there is talk today of cloning humans. However, many scientists think that human cloning would be very risky, and some people believe that cloning of humans should never be carried out. In this book you can learn about genetic engineering and decide for yourself what you think about this controversial area of science.

What is a gene?

In the simplest terms, a **gene** is an inherited instruction for a particular characteristic. Each **organism** inherits its genes from its parents. For instance, genes control the colour of your eyes and the type of hair you have – whether it is straight or curly, fair or dark. Each organism has thousands of genes. Some characteristics are influenced by one or two genes. Eye colour, for example, is influenced by just a few different genes. Other characteristics, such as the height of an individual or their intelligence, are the result of the combined effects of many different genes.

Each gene is a part of a very long molecule found in all living cells, called **DNA** (**deoxyribonucleic acid**). In cells with a **nucleus** (**eukaryote** cells), DNA is found within the nucleus. When the cell is dividing, the individual DNA molecules coil up to form structures called **chromosomes**.

Mutations

Each time a cell divides, it makes a copy of its DNA. On rare occasions a mistake is made and part of the DNA molecule is copied incorrectly. These mistakes in the DNA molecule are called **mutations**. Altered, or mutated, genes can be passed on from a parent to its children.

A child inherits genes from its father and from its mother. The same colour eyes or hair as a parent is a result of these genetic connections.

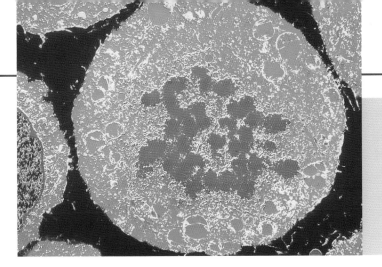

The chromosomes (orange) are clearly visible in the centre of the dividing cell. In non-dividing cells, the chromosomes are not visible. Magnification approx. x 4000.

Most times these changes are small and don't matter much – it would be as if you misspelled a single word in a set of instructions and no one really noticed. Other times, however, the change might alter the whole meaning of a genetic instruction, with the result that the gene does something entirely different. The result may be disastrous, leading to the death of the organism. Then again the change might be harmless – for instance producing straight instead of curly hair. On rare occasions the change gives an advantage. An animal might end up being able to run faster, for example, and so escape from its predators.

Random shuffling

We all have a different set of genes, that play a part in making us who we are. You will have characteristics in common with your parents, and your brothers and other close relations because you have many genes in common, but in each person the mix of genes is different. Only identical twins have exactly the same set of genes.

On the whole, everyone has two versions of each gene, one from each parent. Males and females each produce sex cells – cells that contain only one version of each gene. When these sex cells form, there is some shuffling of the genes. The genes in the parent's chromosomes are mixed into new combinations.

A male and a female sex cell combine in a process called fertilization. The fertilized cell – the first cell of a new living thing – once more has two sets of genes, one from each parent. Fertilization is a random event. There is no plan as to which male and female sex cells will successfully combine to form a new living thing.

The possible number of combinations that can arise from gene shuffling and random fertilization is truly mind-boggling. There are 10^{600} possible gene combinations that can occur in humans. That is a 1 with 600 zeroes after it. Part of what genetic engineering is about is taking the randomness out of the gene shuffling and taking control of which genes appear in a particular organism. Before we get to that, we'll take a closer look at how genes actually work.

2 Reading the manual

A cell's **DNA** can be thought of as an instruction manual – a set of instructions for making parts of a cell. Each **gene** is the plan for a particular part. The parts that genes carry instructions for are called **proteins**. If the instruction written in a gene is acted upon, the result will be that a protein is made.

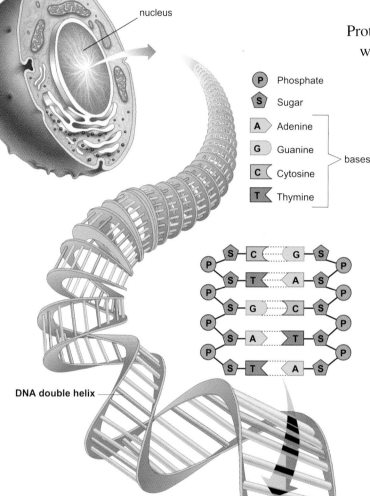

cell

nucleus

P Phosphate
S Sugar
A Adenine
G Guanine
C Cytosine
T Thymine
} bases

DNA double helix

The structure of the DNA molecule. DNA is made up of two long chains of nucleotides, linked at regular intervals and twisted to form a double helix.

Proteins are the building blocks and workhorses of the cell. Some proteins are parts of the cell structure. Others are **enzymes**, **catalysts** that control chemical reactions in the cell. Each reaction in the cell has its own specific enzyme, and because the enzymes control the reactions, they effectively control the cell and the way it develops.

These events at the level of the cell give rise to the characteristics we see in the **organism**, such as pink flowers on a pea plant, or curly hair on a child. This process of acting out a gene's instructions is called **gene expression**.

A cell doesn't act on all its DNA instructions at once. Different genes are switched on and off as they are needed. This is because DNA isn't just a small instruction manual – it's a cellular encyclopedia. You never read an encyclopedia from cover to cover, you only read those articles that you need at a particular time. In a multicellular organism, such as a plant or an animal, all the cells (except the sex cells we mentioned earlier) contain the same DNA. However, there are many different types of cell, and different genes are switched on in each cell type. Every cell in an organism has the same instruction manual, but different cells are reading different parts of it.

DNA and proteins

We have seen that the aim of carrying out a gene's instruction is to make a protein. Protein molecules are long chains, made up of small subunits called **amino acids**. There are 20 or so different kinds of amino acid. A single chain of amino acids is called a **polypeptide**. A protein may have just one polypeptide, or it may have several linked together.

The order of the amino acids in a polypeptide chain is important. Changing one type of amino acid for another can affect the way the protein works. This is why it is so important for the cell to follow the instructions for each protein in its DNA.

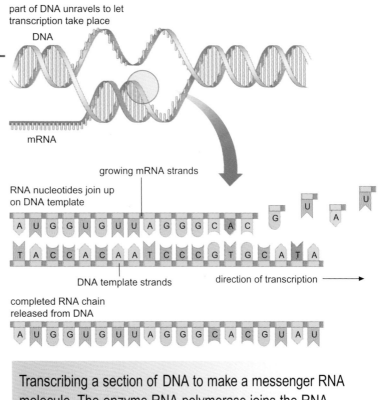

part of DNA unravels to let transcription take place

DNA

mRNA

growing mRNA strands

RNA nucleotides join up on DNA template

DNA template strands

direction of transcription

completed RNA chain released from DNA

Transcribing a section of DNA to make a messenger RNA molecule. The enzyme RNA polymerase joins the RNA nucleotides together to form a single molecule. Transcription happens very quickly: about 30 new nucleotides are added to the chain each second.

A gene's instructions are 'written' in the structure of the DNA molecule. DNA is made up of two long chains of smaller molecules called **nucleotides**. It looks something like a spiralling, twisted ladder, with the two chains wound around each other. Linking the strands together at regular intervals are chemicals called **bases**. It is the order of the bases that carries the genetic instructions.

There are four different bases: adenine (A), cytosine (C), guanine (G) and thymine (T). The bases pair up across the molecule, like rungs on a ladder. T is always paired with A, and G with C. The two DNA chains are said to be complementary because the sequence of bases on one strand determines the sequence on the other.

Copying a gene

When a cell wants to make a particular protein, it first has to copy the instructions from the DNA. Copying a gene is called **transcription**. When a gene is being transcribed, the DNA molecule unwinds at the place where that gene is located. One strand of the DNA, called the coding strand, acts as a template for making another molecule, called **RNA** (**ribonucleic acid**). RNA is very similar to DNA, but it is made up of a single strand of bases, not a double strand. Also, one of the bases in DNA, thymine (T), is replaced by another base called uracil (U). This RNA transcript is called **messenger RNA**. It will carry the protein-building instructions from the **nucleus** to the **cytoplasm** where the actual assembly of bases takes place.

Protein factories

The next stage in making a protein is called **translation**. The order of the **bases** along the **RNA** strand will be translated into a series of **amino acids** to be assembled into a **polypeptide** chain.

But how can just four bases carry instructions for twenty different amino acids? The answer is that the bases have to be 'read' in groups of three. Each group of three bases, called a triplet or **codon**, stands for a particular amino acid. There are 64 possible codons that can be made using four bases. Each amino acid is coded for by one or more of these codons. The amino acid lysine, for instance, can be coded as either AAA or AAG. The complete amino acid dictionary is what we call the **genetic code**. The genetic code is the same in all living **organisms**, a fact that is of great importance in genetic engineering.

Reading the code

The actual process of building proteins takes place in structures called **ribosomes**. Here, the **messenger RNA** is translated codon by codon to produce a polypeptide. A ribosome attaches to a messenger RNA strand at one end. The ribosome travels along the strand, translating it codon by codon.

Another type of RNA, called **transfer RNA**, plays a vital part in the assembly. There are different forms of transfer RNA, each of which carries a particular amino acid. A particular transfer RNA molecule will bind only to the messenger RNA codon that corresponds to the amino acid it carries. For example, a transfer RNA carrying lysine might only bind to the codon AAA.

This illustration shows how proteins (developing polypeptide chains) are assembled on a ribosome. The messenger RNA is translated by transfer RNA.

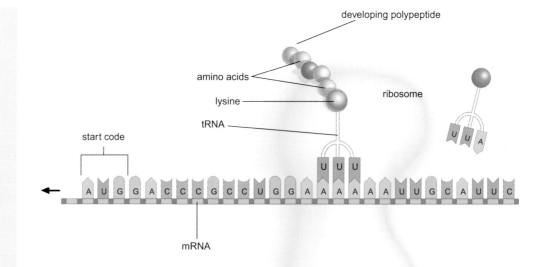

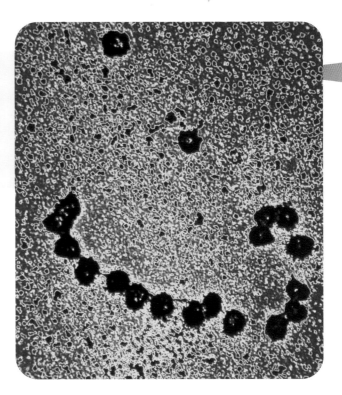

A photo taken through an electron microscope showing a number of ribosomes on a single strand of messenger RNA. Magnification approx. x 270,000.

As the ribosome travels along the messenger RNA, a transfer RNA molecule brings the amino acid for a particular codon on the messenger RNA. As each codon is translated, another amino acid is added to the end of the growing polypeptide chain. There can be more than one ribosome moving along a messenger RNA molecule at any one time. In this way there can be polypeptides at different stages of assembly along the messenger RNA strand, just like a factory production line.

At the end of the messenger RNA strand is a special codon called a stop codon. This means 'instructions end – stop assembly'. The polypeptide chain is complete and is released from the ribosome. It will then fold up, perhaps linking with other polypeptides, to form a **protein** that can go on to fulfil its task in the cell.

Engineering goals

Genetic engineers often aim to transfer **genes** from one **organism** to another, or to alter genes within an organism. The point of doing so is to introduce new proteins into the organism, because doing this changes what happens in the cell. Changing the genes is more effective than simply injecting an organism with new proteins. Proteins don't last long, they are broken down and recycled, but once a gene has been 'written' into the **DNA**, its instructions can be read again and again to make new proteins. Since DNA is copied from one generation to the next, from parents to offspring, changes in DNA can be carried over from one generation to the next.

The fact that all organisms use the same genetic code means that we can transfer genes from one species to another, and the new species will be able to read the gene. The universal nature of the genetic code means that any gene can be decoded by any organism and give the same protein product (although there are some problems for bacteria reading **eukaryote** cell genes, as we will see later). Genetic engineers can put human genes in pigs and jellyfish genes in mice.

Gene control

An **organism's** cells, as we have seen, only use some of their **genes**. Different cell types, with their different tasks to perform, require the services of different **proteins**, which have to be constructed according to the instructions on different segments of the cell **DNA**. Some estimates suggest that the cells of a multicellular organism use only 5 to 10 per cent of their genes at any given time. This means that there has to be a control system in place that prevents genes from being expressed here, there and everywhere indiscriminately. A gene that is not expressed has no effect whatsoever on the cell.

Some genes are being expressed all the time because the proteins concerned are involved in vital activities. The **enzymes** involved for instance in **respiration**, the process by which living things get energy from food, are always needed. Other genes may never be expressed at all in a cell, or may be expressed just once in a while according to need. One reason why bacteria are such phenomenally successful organisms is that they can rapidly step up or cut back on the production of enzymes, depending on the nutrients that become available to them.

Regulatory proteins

The control of **gene expression** is very complex. Genes can be switched on or off by special proteins called **regulatory proteins**. Often several different regulatory proteins can act on one gene. They may act on the gene site itself to allow **transcription**, or they may block it. They may act at a later stage in the process, controlling production of a **polypeptide** by the **ribosomes**. Finally they may affect the actual polypeptides produced, either activating or deactivating them in some way.

The genes that code for production of blossoms in these cherry trees are not expressed until environmental factors, such as day length, act as a trigger. This means that all the cherry trees in an area blossom at the same time, making it much easier for trees to pollinate each other.

One very simple example of gene regulation was discovered in bacteria over 30 years ago. A series of genes in the bacteria (lac genes) produce enzymes that can break down the sugar **lactose** (this provides the bacterium with energy). When there is no lactose available, a regulatory protein called a repressor binds to the bacterial DNA and stops the genes from being transcribed. However, the repressor protein is made inactive by lactose, which stops the repressor from binding to the bacterial DNA. Thus if there is lactose in the bacterial cell, transcription of the lac genes can go ahead. The lac genes then produce enzymes that the bacterium can use to get energy from the lactose.

Promoters

Like other reactions in the cell, the production of **messenger RNA** (see illustration on page 7) from a particular stretch of DNA is controlled by an **enzyme**. Before this enzyme can go to work, it must attach to the DNA at a point just before the gene. This site is called a **promoter**. When the enzyme is bound to the promoter site, the gene can be transcribed to produce messenger RNA. Without the enzyme, transcription is not possible.

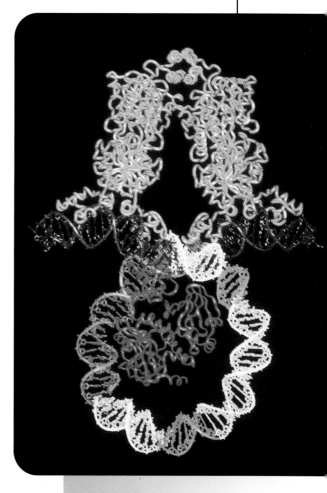

Unlike the **genetic code** itself, promoters are not universal. Some promoters work in more than one species, but in some cases the enzyme of one species does not recognize and bind to the promoter in another. If this happens there will be no transcription and so no **protein** building: the gene will not be expressed.

If a genetic engineer wants to transfer a gene from one organism to another, the section of DNA they transfer must include the promoter as well as the gene itself. Furthermore, the promoter must be recognized by the binding enzymes in the host organism's cells. If these conditions are not met, nothing will happen.

A computer graphic showing the (pink) lac repressor protein attached to the DNA. The sites at which it attaches stops the enzyme RNA polymerase, a promoter, from attaching to the DNA. Magnification approx. x 40,000.

Some bacteria used in genetic research have enzymes that will readily bind to promoters from a range of other organisms. Other bacteria are quite fussy about the promoters they will respond to.

3 Bacterial benefits

The first successes in genetic engineering involved inserting foreign genes into bacteria. This might not seem very useful – bacteria are extremely small, very simple **organisms**. However, genetically engineered bacteria have been useful in several different ways.

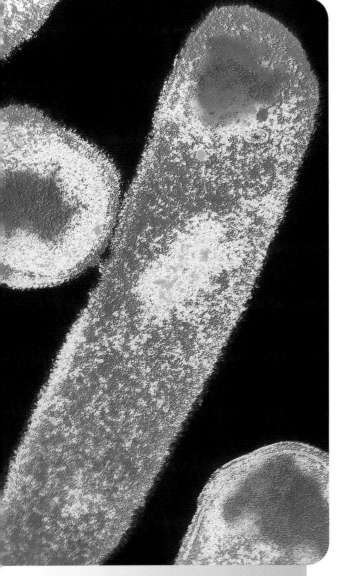

These *Bacillus subtilis* bacteria have been genetically modified to produce a vaccine. The red and purple coloured areas in the bacteria indicate the presence of the vaccine. Magnification approx. x 50,000.

Humans have a long history of using bacteria for a variety of tasks. Bacteria are involved in the production of yoghurt and cheese, for example. We also get **antibiotics**, the drugs we use to fight off infections, from bacteria. Bacteria have been engaged in chemical warfare with one another for many millions of years. Antibiotics are part of this battle. An antibiotic is a substance that kills or prevents the growth of bacteria. Soil bacteria in particular produce antibiotics as part of their natural defences, to kill off other bacterial colonies growing in the same area.

Hundreds of different antibiotics obtained from a variety of **micro-organisms** are in use today. The search for new ones continues as medical science tries to keep pace with the ability of bacteria to evolve rapidly and gain resistance to everything we can throw at them.

Building better bugs

One aim of the genetic engineer is to make bacteria that can do the things we want to do even better. A method used in the past was the hit-and-miss approach of artificially causing **mutations** in a colony of bacteria and hoping that some desirable mutation would occur. A more certain way is to isolate **genes** that produce **proteins** we are interested in and insert them directly into the bacteria we wish to alter. The ability of populations of bacteria to grow rapidly makes them extremely good chemical factories for the production of useful proteins.

Drugs from bugs

One protein made in genetically engineered bacteria is used to treat **diabetes**. Diabetes is a potentially serious illness caused by an inability to produce a hormone called insulin. Insulin is a protein that is involved in controlling the amount of sugar in the blood. Without it, levels of sugar in the blood may vary wildly, causing all kinds of problems. In the days before genetic engineering, diabetics were treated with insulin obtained from pigs and cattle. This was not an ideal treatment because insulin from these animals is slightly different from human insulin. Today, stainless steel vats hold vast populations of *Escherichia coli* bacteria (*E. coli* for short) that have been genetically altered to contain the genes for human insulin. These bacteria were the first large-scale use of genetically engineered organisms. Today, other medically important proteins are also manufactured by bacteria, including blood-clotting agents, growth hormones and interferon (a protein that is effective against infections caused by **viruses**).

As yet, scientists have not been able to genetically engineer bacteria to produce antibiotics. Antibiotics are not proteins, so it is not possible to simply insert an 'antibiotic gene' into a bacterium. Instead, genetic engineers would have to insert most or all of the genes that code for the **enzymes** involved in making the antibiotic.

Clean-up squad

Genetically altered bacteria may also be used to deal with pollution. Many bacteria play a vital role as decomposers, breaking down dead organisms and recycling organic wastes, making nutrients available for reuse by other living things. Researchers have been able to genetically engineer bacteria that can also break down oil spills and neutralize harmful chemicals that cause pollution. However, until now these bacteria have only been tested in the laboratory. If they prove to be safe, such bacteria could be an effective way of cleaning up environmental hazards.

These fermentation vessels are used to grow huge numbers of micro-organisms that have been genetically altered to produce substances such as insulin.

4 Inserting new genes

We have learnt about some of the useful jobs that genetically engineered bacteria are doing for us. But how exactly are these bacteria made? How do genetic engineers put new **genes** into bacteria?

Introducing *E. coli*

E. coli is a common bacterium that lives in the intestines of mammals, including humans. It is mostly harmless and is very easy to keep in the laboratory. Given ideal conditions it can divide in two every 40 minutes or so. For many years *E. coli* has been studied by scientists, and the many genetic engineering techniques were developed using this **organism**.

Eukaryote and prokaryote chromosomes

Like all other bacteria, *E. coli* is a **prokaryote**. This means that it has no **nucleus**. The cells of all other living things are **eukaryotes**.

The genetic material in bacteria is in some ways different from that in eukaryotes. In eukaryote cells, **DNA** is bound up with **proteins** called **histones**. A single molecule of DNA is wound around a number of histones in a complex fashion, making it compact and able to fit inside the nucleus. The DNA is at its most compact during cell division, when the DNA and histone structure becomes visible under the microscope as a **chromosome**.

In a prokaryote cell, the DNA is 'naked' – it is not enclosed within a nucleus or associated with proteins to form a chromosome. The prokaryote 'chromosome' is simply a DNA molecule folded up inside the cell. The ends of prokaryote DNA molecules are joined, forming a closed loop of DNA. Eukaryote chromosomes do not form loops like this.

There are around 4 million base pairs in the DNA molecule of *E. coli*. This is tiny compared to the 100 million base pairs in a single human chromosome (humans have 23 pairs of chromosomes in each cell). When *E. coli* reproduces, its single chromosome loop is replicated and each new bacterium gets a copy.

A magnified photo of the rod-shaped *E. coli* bacteria. Magnification approx. x 5000.

Plasmids

As well as its single DNA molecule, *E. coli* may also have a few smaller loops of DNA called **plasmids**, which can also be passed on at cell division. Plasmids have only a few thousand base pairs. There are various types of plasmid, but generally a bacterium will have only one type at any one time. However, it can have many copies of the same plasmid. It is not unusual for a bacterium to have hundreds of identical plasmids. Sometimes a bacterium can have no plasmids at all, which suggests that plasmids are not essential for the bacterium's survival.

The genes on plasmids are often ones that give the bacterium resistance to **antibiotics**, which we have seen are used by bacteria to wage war on other bacterial strains. A bacterium that has plasmids will be resistant to attack by antibiotic-producing bacteria.

Plasmids are important in genetic engineering because they can be extracted from bacterial cells. They can then be readily introduced into bacterial cells that have no plasmids of their own. Plasmid genes can therefore be introduced into bacteria that previously did not have any.

The discovery of the techniques for transferring plasmids from cell to cell was an important step in the development of genetic engineering but it was only the beginning. A major factor in the advance of genetic engineering came with the discovery of another weapon that bacteria use to defend themselves against attack. This weapon is a special class of **enzymes** that the bacteria use to chop up the DNA of an attacking **virus**. They are called **restriction enzymes**.

The loops in this photo are plasmids inside an *E. coli* bacterium. Magnification approx. x 80,000.

Chopping up DNA

Multicellular animals are vulnerable to attack by **micro-organisms**. This means that they have had to evolve some form of defence against infection. The human **immune system** includes millions of white blood cells, which can identify foreign invaders and then use various methods to deal with them.

Bacteria, microscopically small though they are, are themselves liable to infection by even smaller disease-causing agents – **viruses**. Viruses that infect bacteria are called **bacteriophages**, often shortened to simply phages. The phages inject their **DNA** into bacterial cells.

Bacteria have a type of defence system to help fight against viral attack, but the bacterial defence system is nothing like our complex immune system. After all, a tiny single-celled **organism** cannot call on millions of white blood cells to go on the offensive against the invader. Instead, **enzymes** in the bacterium recognize the presence of foreign viral DNA, and other enzymes go to work to chop it into pieces.

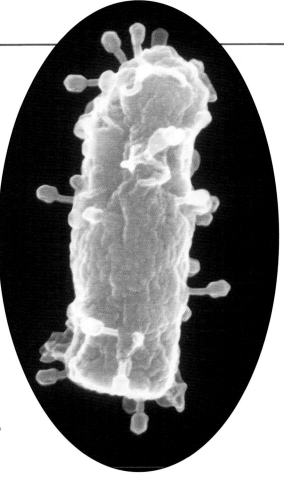

A scanning electron micrograph of T4 bacteriophages on an *E. coli* bacterium. The restriction enzymes that bacteria use to cut open viral DNA are used by genetic engineers to cut DNA into fragments. Magnification approx. x 31,000.

The enzymes responsible for chopping up the viral DNA are called **restriction enzymes**. Each type of restriction enzyme recognizes a short sequence of DNA bases, called its target sequence. If a foreign DNA molecule has these target sequences, the restriction enzyme will cut through the DNA molecule and split it into fragments. Each fragment is roughly speaking a 'gene-sized' piece of DNA around 1000 to 5000 base pairs in length, just large enough for one or a few genes.

Restriction enzymes and genetic engineering

It is possible to remove restriction enzymes from bacteria and purify them in the laboratory. Many hundreds of enzymes from many strains of bacteria have been isolated and these make up the genetic engineers' 'toolkit'. They can be used for cutting up DNA, and therefore for cutting out genes. Restriction enzymes are what make possible a genetic engineering technique called **recombinant DNA** technology. Using this technique the genetic engineer can combine DNA from different species.

Recombinant DNA technology is the basis of genetic engineering. Restriction enzymes are used to cut up the DNA from one organism, and genes of interest are isolated from the fragments. Restriction enzymes are then used to open **plasmids**, and the genes isolated from the first organism are inserted into the opened plasmid. The plasmid is then closed up, to produce a plasmid with a foreign **gene** inserted into it. This technique is called **gene splicing**. Plasmids containing foreign DNA are called recombinant plasmids.

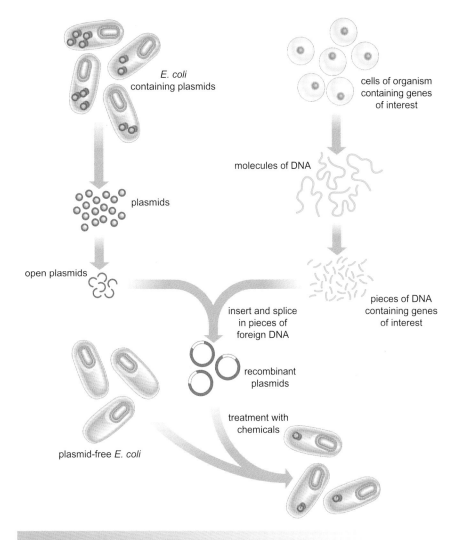

E. coli containing plasmids

cells of organism containing genes of interest

molecules of DNA

plasmids

open plasmids

insert and splice in pieces of foreign DNA

pieces of DNA containing genes of interest

recombinant plasmids

treatment with chemicals

plasmid-free *E. coli*

Using restriction enzymes, DNA can be cut into gene-sized fragments. Other enzymes are used to insert the DNA fragments into bacterial plasmids. Bacterial cells are then treated with chemicals to help them take up the engineered plasmids.

A suspension of bacteria is then treated with the recombinant plasmids. Some of the bacteria take up the plasmids. The suspension is spread on the surface of a growth medium (a jelly-like substance, called **agar gel**, that contains nutrients that the bacteria can use as food), and the bacteria begin to divide. As the bacteria go on dividing there will soon be a population of genetically identical individuals, **clones** in other words, all containing a copy of the recombinant plasmid.

The plasmids act as carriers for transferring genes into bacteria. These genes can come from any source. They might come from another bacterium, either of the same or another species, or they might come from an entirely different organism such as a plant or an animal.

Split genes

When **DNA** and **genes** were first being investigated, it was assumed that each gene was a continuous section of DNA that could be read and transcribed to give a continuous corresponding length of **messenger RNA**. This would then be translated to give the appropriate series of **amino acids** to be linked together in a **polypeptide** chain. However, scientists were surprised to find that the truth was a little more complicated.

Cross-section of an animal cell which has been cultured (grown) in the laboratory. Cells like this are used to produce messenger RNA, from which complementary DNA (cDNA) can be made.

There is a major difference between the structure of **eukaryote** genes and **prokaryote** genes. Many genes in eukaryote cells are not a continuous sequence of DNA, but are split over several segments. The DNA is not physically split: the long chain of the molecule remains intact. However, the **protein-**making code that makes up the gene is interrupted by sequences of bases that do not code for proteins. These non-coding regions within the gene are called **introns**, because they interrupt the code. The coding regions of the DNA are called **exons**. Not all eukaryote genes are split, but some are split spectacularly. The gene for collagen, a protein found in animal tissues such as tendons, is interrupted by nearly 40 introns.

The intron sections of the gene obviously have to be removed before the messenger RNA can be used to manufacture a protein chain. This happens after the messenger RNA has been made from the DNA, but before it leaves the **nucleus**. **Enzymes** cut out the RNA sequences that correspond to the introns and connect the exon sections together again. Once the messenger RNA has been modified, it passes out of the nucleus for translation into a polypeptide.

Bacterial genes have no introns. Each gene is a continuous stretch of DNA code, with no interruptions. This raises a problem for the genetic engineer. If a eukaryote gene is transferred to a bacterium and if that gene happens to a be a split gene, there is no way in which the bacterium can produce a protein from that gene. The bacterium has no machinery for modifying RNA and removing introns from it. If genetic engineers want to introduce a eukaryote gene into a bacterium, they have first to find a way of making the split gene usable.

Intron bypass operation

The solution to the problem is to transfer genes that have already had their introns removed. Simply, the eukaryote cells from which the genes are being removed are made to do most of the work. Rather than cutting up a cell's DNA to get the target gene, the genetic engineer looks for the messenger RNA strand corresponding to the gene in the **cytoplasm** of the cell. Such an RNA strand will already have had the introns removed before leaving the nucleus. Once the messenger RNA has been isolated, it is used as a template to produce a complementary strand of DNA (cDNA). This cDNA strand is equivalent to the gene minus its introns.

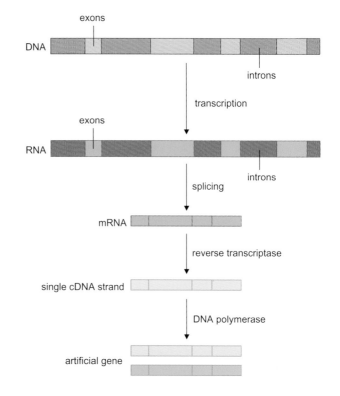

Copying the RNA to give cDNA is the reverse of what happens during **transcription**: instead of DNA being used to make messenger RNA, messenger RNA is used to make DNA. Scientists can get this reverse transcription to take place in the laboratory thanks to the discovery of an enzyme found in some **viruses**. This enzyme is called, appropriately enough, **reverse transcriptase**.

Reverse transcriptase has the very useful property that when it is brought into contact with a messenger RNA strand and a source of **nucleotides** (the building blocks of DNA), it will assemble a DNA strand that complements the sequence of bases on the RNA. This single DNA strand can then be used as a template to make a

How complementary DNA (cDNA) is made, containing only the exons of a eukaryote gene.

second DNA strand, by using the services of another enzyme called **DNA polymerase**. The end result is an artificial gene that contains a continuous sequence of coding bases, without the introns.

The artificial gene can be spliced into a **plasmid**, which can be inserted into a bacterium. Once there, it can start to produce proteins.

Hitting the target

We have seen how it is possible to move **DNA** from one **organism** to another, but how does the genetic engineer ensure that the right DNA segment is being introduced? How can specific genes be isolated and transferred?

Gene libraries

The complete set of **genes** in an organism is called its **genome**. There are around 400 genes in the *E. coli* genome, and over 30,000 genes in the human genome. When genetic engineers want to isolate a gene, they split up the entire genome of a cell containing that gene, and incorporate the gene fragments into bacteria via **plasmids**. Each of the individual genes from the cell will end up in a separate bacterium. This mixed collection of genetically altered bacteria make up a gene library of the original organism.

Dishes of agar gel containing colonies of bacteria that contain recombinant genes.

So we know that the gene we are interested in is somewhere among thousands of genetically modified bacteria, but how do we find it?

Gene screening

The first step in finding the gene we want is to spread out the bacteria on a suitable growing medium, such as an **agar gel** containing nutrients. The individual bacteria will then divide, and each one will form a colony containing millions of bacteria. The individuals in each colony will be **clones** of the original bacterium. It is easier to test a colony of clones for a particular gene than it is to attempt to test a single tiny bacterium.

It is tricky to look for the gene we want to find directly, but it is often possible to look for the **protein** it produces. If the bacteria in a colony are producing a protein, they must have the gene or genes that code for that protein.

If the protein concerned is an **enzyme**, it is reasonably straightforward to find it. Every enzyme controls a particular chemical reaction in the cell. If we provide each bacterial colony with a sample of the enzyme's **substrate** (the chemical that the enzyme interacts with), we can then test each colony for the products of the reaction.

If the protein product is not an enzyme, there are still ways in which it can be detected. Antibodies are proteins that are produced by the **immune systems** of vertebrates. They are designed to detect foreign proteins and bind to them, to help neutralize them. Each antibody is specific to a particular intruder, so it is possible to produce antibodies that are specific to a particular protein. The antibody becomes our protein detector. We can use the antibody to screen the bacterial colonies for the protein we want to find.

Gene probes

Another method of finding genes involves the use of **gene probes**. Every type of gene is unique. Each gene has a sequence of base pairs found in no other gene, and it is this feature that the genetic engineer uses to identify it. A short stretch of DNA is made that matches up with a unique part of the gene we are trying to find. This is the gene probe. The probe is 'labelled' using a **radioactive** material. The DNA in the probe will bind to the gene we are hunting for and to no other.

First, a small sample of each colony is transferred to a nylon filter. These sample colonies are then treated with a strong chemical that disrupts the bacterial cells, causing them to release their DNA. The chemical also causes the two strands of each DNA molecule to separate from one another. The filter is treated to remove any traces of protein, and the single-stranded DNA is 'baked' in place. The filter now has DNA prints (sometimes called DNA ghosts) of all the colonies being tested.

To find out which DNA print the probe has bound to, the filter is brought into contact with a sheet of X-ray film. The radioactivity from the label on the probe will cause a dark spot to appear on the film, indicating where the colony we are interested in is located.

An X-ray plate used in gene probe detection. The dark spots on the plate are fragments of human chromosome 17. A defective version of this gene is associated with breast cancer.

Turning to phages again

We first met **bacteriophages**, the **viruses** that attack bacteria, when we looked at **restriction enzymes** – the bacterium's defence against virus attack. Restriction enzymes have proved to be a powerful tool for the genetic engineer, but so too are the phages themselves, as well as other types of virus.

Phage delivery systems

Bacteriophages and other types of virus work by inserting their **DNA** into a host cell, and hijacking the cell machinery to make copies of the virus. The host cell makes copies of the viral DNA, and transcribes the viral genes to make the **proteins** that form the virus's outer coat. The viral proteins and DNA are assembled into new viruses. This is the only way a virus can reproduce – outside a host cell it is to all intents and purposes lifeless.

Genetic engineers can use **phages** as carriers, instead of **plasmids**, to insert foreign DNA into bacterial cells. As with plasmids, restriction enzymes can be used to cut open the DNA and splice in new **genes**. The **recombinant viruses** formed are then used to infect a colony of bacteria. Each phage infects a bacterium and reproduces inside it. The new phages that are formed contain copies of the inserted gene. Eventually the bacterial cell is so full of viral copies that it splits open. The released phages go on to infect other bacteria in the colony, until there are billions of copies of the recombinant viruses. The viruses containing the genes we are interested in can then be isolated.

One advantage of inserting genes using phages rather than plasmids is that phages can be made to carry longer lengths of foreign DNA than plasmids can. Phages are often used to construct gene libraries because the DNA needs to be split into fewer fragments, meaning that fewer colonies of **clones** need to be made. This makes it easier to find the bacterial colony containing the protein we are looking for.

The DNA of a bacteriophage,
Magnification approx. x 50,000.

22

Other hosts

Although *E. coli* was the first host cell used by genetic researchers it is by no means the only one. No cell is immune from virus attack and so viruses can be used to carry foreign DNA into any type of cell, **prokaryote** or **eukaryote**.

It is possible to modify viruses to transfer genes into the host cell's own DNA, instead of making new viruses. When the host cell divides, it not only replicates its own DNA but also the recombinant viral DNA that has been added to it.

Sometimes a virus can take on a plasmid-like existence inside the host cell, replicating its DNA plus the spliced in foreign genes independently of the host cell's **chromosomes**. These 'plasmids' are then passed on to the next generation when the host cell divides. No virus particles are produced and the host cell is unharmed.

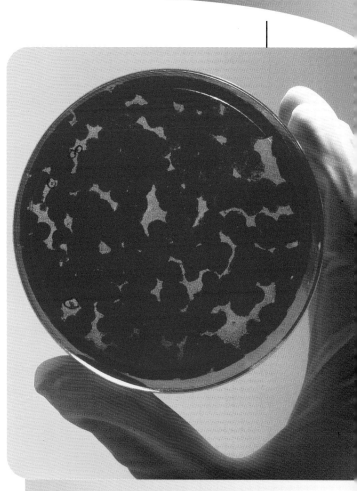

This tissue culture of skin provides a way of testing new drugs without using living organisms.

Stepping up

So far we have only discussed genetically altering single cells. Mostly this is done in order to set up microbe 'factories' that will produce a protein that we want to have in large quantities, such as insulin for example. Alternatively it might be done to 'improve' a cell, making a bacterium a more efficient consumer of petrochemical wastes, for instance, or altering yeast cells to make them more efficient producers of beer or wine.

Animal and plant cells can be grown in tissue cultures, by taking cells from plant and animal tissues and growing them in the laboratory. These tissue cultures can also be genetically engineered. Animal tissue cultures are used in the production of **vaccines** for some viruses, for example. However, this is quite different from producing genetically engineered multicellular **organisms**. Next we will look at the techniques involved in producing genetically modified plants and animals.

5 Going multicellular

In some ways, the methods used to genetically engineer multicellular plants and animals are similar to those used for single-celled **organisms**. Of course, there are differences between the two. A multicellular organism is made up of many millions of cells. To change the **genome** of a multicellular organism we need to have a way of introducing the new genes into every one of its cells in such a way that the new genes are passed on when cell division takes place.

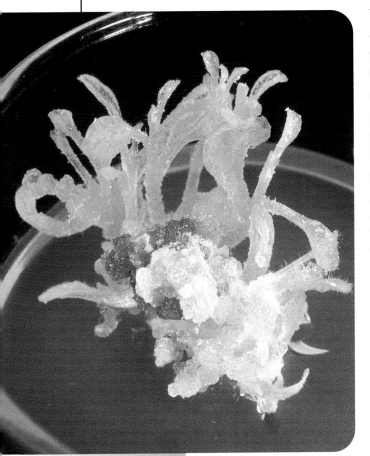

These plantlets of the tobacco plant (*Nicotinia tabacum*) were grown from callus cells. Each callus cell has the potential to form a complete new plant.

We also want the change to be passed on from generation to generation when the organism reproduces. Most living things reproduce sexually, not by simply dividing like a bacterium. This means that offspring inherit their **genes** from two parents. Each parent forms special sex cells, called **gametes**, with half the number of genes, which combine to form a new organism. Any altered **DNA** needs to be present in these gametes if it is to be passed on to the offspring.

It has already been mentioned that, although each cell in a multicellular organism carries the same genes, not all genes are expressed (active) at all times or in all cells. It is therefore important that any introduced genes are in the right place. We would not want the foreign gene to be expressed unnecessarily, or perhaps not expressed at all. For example, if we introduced a gene into a plant that improved water uptake by the roots, we would want to avoid having the plant wasting the energy by having its leaves pointlessly producing the protein as well.

Plant regeneration

Plants have a remarkable ability to regenerate themselves. A single cell or small pieces of plant tissue can be persuaded to grow into a whole plant. One way of doing this is from a clump of cells called a **callus**. A callus is a group of **undifferentiated** plant cells – cells that are all the same and have no specialized functions. The cells in a callus are attached to each other, they are not a colony of single cells, but they can be separated out from

These vanilla plants (*Vanilla plantifolia*) are clones. They have been grown from the cells of a single parent plant.

each other. Given the right conditions, each cell will form a new callus. Each new callus can then be treated with plant hormones and encouraged to grow into a new plantlet. When these plantlets are planted out and allowed to grow, they develop into mature plants. In this way many **clones** of a single plant can be produced.

Producing plant clones in this way has many advantages over growing plants from seed. Plants with superior characteristics, such as larger fruits, can be cloned in this way. All the clones will share the original plant's characteristics. Although this is one way of taking control of the reproduction of the plant in order to gain a particular result, it is highly selective breeding rather than real genetic engineering.

The advantage of generating plant clones from the genetic engineer's point of view is simple. If we can insert foreign genes into a group of callus cells, then it is reasonably straightforward to produce genetically altered mature plants from these cells. There remains the problem of getting the foreign genes into the callus cells. In fact, nature has got there ahead of us, and genetic engineers have been able to take advantage of an existing mechanism for getting genes into callus cells.

Nature's genetic engineer

Many plants, such as potatoes, beans and most trees can be affected by a condition called crown gall disease. This causes a lump, or **gall**, to appear at the site of a wound. The cause of the disease is a soil bacterium called *Agrobacterium tumefaciens*.

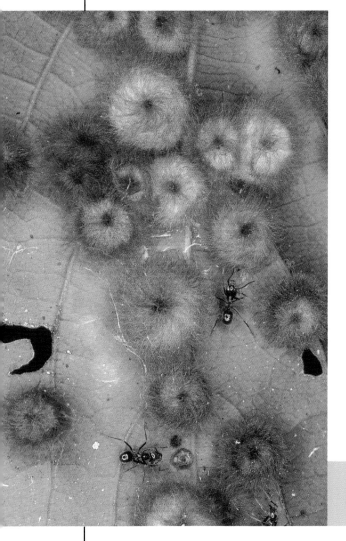

A gall is a mass of **undifferentiated** plant cells, like a **callus**. It is like a cancer tumour in a person: a mass of cells growing out of control. Even when the callus is removed from the plant and cultivated in the laboratory away from the bacterium, it remains tumourous. The tumour cells make substances called **opines** which are not found in normal plant cells.

Agrobacterium tumefaciens uses opines as its main nutrient and source of energy. Only this bacterium can make use of opines in this way; other soil microbes lack the **enzymes** needed to break down opines. So only this particular species of bacterium gains an advantage from the plant tumour. What the bacterium does when it infects a plant is to genetically engineer the plant cells to produce tumourous cells, which provide it with a source of food.

Crown galls on the underside of damaged leaves of a rainforest tree.

The return of the plasmids

Agrobacterium tumefaciens uses **plasmids** to cause, or induce, tumours in the plant. These are called **Ti** (tumour-inducing) **plasmids**. The bacterium causes healthy plant cells to change into opine-producing tumour cells by transferring Ti plasmids into them. Once the Ti plasmid has been introduced into the plant cell, part of it becomes integrated into the plant cell's **DNA**. The plasmid DNA transferred to the plant contains genes that code for **proteins** involved in gall formation and another **gene** that is needed for making opines. The bacterium has effectively achieved with the plant cells what genetic engineers have been doing with bacteria. It has converted them into factories to produce a product it can use.

It is not too much of a problem for the genetic engineer to latch on to the success of the *Agrobacterium* in transferring DNA from one species to another. It is a fairly straightforward procedure to snip out the genes in the plasmid that cause tumour formation and replace them with genes that do things that we want. The genetically altered bacterium is then used to infect plant tissue and the foreign genes are taken into the plant's DNA as before. It is not necessary to infect every cell in a plant because whole plants can be regenerated from infected cells in the same way as they are grown from callus cells.

In nature, *Agrobacterium tumefaciens* only infects those plants that belong to the group called dicotyledons, or **dicots**. These are plants that have two leaves, called **cotyledons**, in the seed. They include beans, peas and potatoes. Many vital food crops, such as rice and wheat, are **monocots** (they have a single seed-leaf). Genetic engineers are working on ways of altering the bacterium to make it infect monocotyledons as well as dicotyledons.

Expressing the new genes

It is not enough just to transfer the genes producing the desired protein into the plant. Plant genes are often controlled by sequences of DNA next to the gene. These sequences need to be included with the gene if it is to be expressed in the plant cell. It is possible, by attaching the right control sequences, to have any gene expressed in any plant tissue.

Agrobacterium tumefaciens bacteria growing on the surface of tobacco plant cells. These bacteria inject cancer-causing genes into a plant cell. The resulting tumour is destructive to the plant, but is food for the bacteria. Magnification approx. x 26,000.

Designer plants

Using *Agrobacterium tumefaciens* is not the only way in which to get new **genes** into plants. Other means include getting the plant cells to take up the foreign **DNA** directly, in the same way that bacterial cells can be made to take up **plasmids**. The difficulty in doing this with a plant cell is that the cell's tough outer wall has to be removed first. This can be done using **enzymes** that break down the cellulose and other materials in the cell wall.

A plant cell with its cell wall removed is called a **protoplast**. Foreign DNA can be introduced into a protoplast using a variety of techniques, such as using electric shocks and chemicals. After the new genes have been introduced, the protoplasts will regrow their cell walls (this takes about a week). The plant cells can then be regenerated to give genetically engineered plants.

Better plants

Regeneration has not proven to be so successful with **monocot** cereal plants, such as wheat and maize, as it is with **dicots** such as carrots and potatoes. However, it can be done, and genetically engineered rice, maize and other crops are now a reality. Improved varieties that give greater yields have been produced.

Other plants have been genetically engineered to produce less lignin. Lignin is a tough chemical that strengthens plant cell walls in woody tissues. It has to be chemically removed from wood that is used to make paper, so trees engineered to contain less lignin would be very useful to the paper industry.

Plants genetically engineered to be resistant to powerful herbicides (weed killers) are perhaps the most common type of GM (genetically modified) crop. Growing such crops means that farmers can use high levels of herbicides to kill weeds around the crops without harming the crops themselves.

Some people have doubts about the use of genetically modified plants in food. In many countries, research to ensure that such crops are safe is under way.

A grove of golden aspen trees. Aspens are one of the tree species that have been genetically engineered to produce less lignin.

Vitamins and vaccines

Genetic engineers are working on the development of plants that can be used to produce medically useful substances such as vitamins, **vaccines** and human **proteins** such as haemoglobin.

One possibility being explored is to grow plants that have been genetically altered to provide essential vitamins for people in developing countries. Around 400 million people worldwide suffer from vitamin A deficiency, which can lead to infections and blindness. Genetic engineers have succeeded in modifying a total of seven genes from plants, bacteria and fungi and introducing all of them into rice. The result has been to create strains of rice that not only produce the chemical involved in vitamin A formation but also contain large amounts of iron. As little as 300 grams of the cooked improved rice should provide almost all the vitamin A that a person needs each day.

Another area of research is the development of edible plant vaccines. This could become a simple, cost-effective way to combat disease worldwide. If people could simply eat foods that are part of their normal diet, but are genetically enhanced to carry vaccines, this would avoid all the problems and the expense of providing equipment for making, storing and delivering vaccines in poorer countries where they are most needed. Bananas are one possible carrier for these vaccines. Genetically engineered potato plants that **immunize** a person against bacteria that cause diarrhoea have already been successfully grown and tested.

The tomatoes top right are normal, and have begun to go mouldy. The tomatoes below them are the same age, but have been genetically modified to be mould-resistant.

Transgenic animals

Plants or animals that have been genetically altered using foreign genes are said to be **transgenic organisms**. We have seen what methods have been developed to create transgenic plants. Animals, however, do not have a plant's ability to regenerate from a single cell. So how can transgenic animals be created?

Going to work on the egg

Although adult animals are made up of millions of different cells, every animal starts life as a single cell – the fertilized egg or zygote. As the animal grows, whether inside an eggshell or inside its mother, this single cell divides again and again. As more and more cells are formed, they diversify to produce all the various cells and tissues and organs that make up the mature animal. When genetic engineers place a new **gene** or genes into an animal, they want to be sure that every cell in the animal contains the new piece of **DNA**. The simplest way to do this is to add the new DNA to a fertilized egg before it starts to divide. Getting new genes into a fertilized egg involves altering an animal's **gametes** (egg cells in a female, sperm cells in a male). These are the only animal cells capable of giving rise to new offspring. All other cells in an animal are called **somatic cells**. Somatic cells are not capable of regenerating into whole new animals.

The fertilized egg cell of a sea urchin. Any changes made to the DNA of a fertilized egg will be present in every cell of the adult organism. Magnification approx. x 1400.

If the altered DNA is successfully incorporated into a **chromosome** in the **nucleus** of a fertilized egg, it will be copied with the rest of the cell's DNA every time the cell divides. The new DNA will thus be present in every cell of the mature animal. The new DNA may also be present in the mature animal's gametes, and so will be passed on to its offspring.

Micro-injection

One way to produce a transgenic animal is to use a technique called **micro-injection**. Injecting DNA into a fertilized egg is a tricky procedure. Using an ultra-fine needle, the new DNA is injected directly into a fertilized egg cell, the zygote, before it starts dividing.

Micro-injection is far from 100 per cent effective. In most cases the injected DNA will not be incorporated into a chromosome in the zygote, and none of the cells in the resulting organism will have the new DNA. Other problems can arise with micro-injection. Sometimes the new DNA does not get incorporated into a chromosome until after the egg has started to divide. The result is a mosaic animal, which

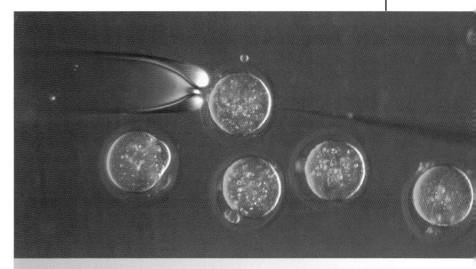

Micro-injection of DNA into an egg cell. The thick tube on the left is a tiny suction tube which holds the cell in one place. The very fine needle on the right is used to inject DNA into the cell. Magnification approx. x 1000.

contains the new gene in some of its cells, but not in others. Another possibility is that the foreign DNA can disrupt the functioning of an important gene in the host cell, so that the animal is weakened or dies.

Micro-injection of DNA cannot be carried out within the animal: it has to be done in the laboratory. Once the DNA has been injected, each egg has to be implanted into the **uterus** of another female of the same species, who will act as a **surrogate mother**. Only a small number of the implanted eggs will develop successfully into mature, healthy individuals.

The time and effort involved in creating transgenic animals means that we cannot simply produce thousands of mature animals and then test each one to see if it is carrying the genes we are interested in. Instead, the gene we want has to be **cloned** in advance, using bacteria or cell cultures to find the gene. Once we have a supply of cloned cells containing the gene we want, they can be used as a source of the gene for micro-injection.

Researchers have developed **transgenic** animals with inherited diseases that are similar to some of those that affect humans. These animals are used by researchers to study the progress and symptoms of a disease. They can also be used to test potential new drugs and treatments more safely and inexpensively than can be done with human volunteers. The majority of the transgenic animals developed for this purpose are mice, because they are small and easy to manipulate and maintain. However, other animals such as rats, rabbits, and pigs have also been used for disease studies.

Ethics and OncoMouse

In 1988 the DuPont pharmaceutical company was granted a patent in the United States on a transgenic mouse called OncoMouse. This mouse had been altered by giving it certain faulty genes, called oncogenes, that ensured that it would develop cancers. OncoMice are now used all over the world to test drugs and therapies against cancer.

Other transgenic animals have since been developed for such diseases as **AIDS**, heart disease and **diabetes**. While the diseases that have been introduced into the mice closely resemble those that appear in humans, there are differences and this limits the suitability of the mice for research into human cancers. Because of these differences, scientists need to be careful about drawing conclusions on the treatment of a human disease based on the study of transgenic animals.

Although, of course, the scientists involved would say that their studies were carried out with the best of intentions, in other words to rid humans of a terrible disease, there are others who would say that is wrong to inflict suffering on animals for the benefit of humans. Genetic engineering also raises ethical questions on broader issues such as whether or not we have any right to 'interfere with nature' by designing 'new' **organisms**. The idea of patenting an animal and claiming rights of ownership over it also upsets many people.

This new-born genetically modified mouse contains jellyfish genes that manufacture a protein called GFP (green fluorescent protein). The GFP makes the mouse glow green. It is hoped that GFP can be used to mark cancer cells, in order to study them.

Research in genetics

Transgenic organisms have been developed to allow scientists to study the structure of **genes** and how they work. They are used to study gene function by seeing what effects specific genetic changes have on the characteristics of the whole animal. Transgenic zebra fish are used to study how genes are activated during the development of the **embryo**. Human and fish development actually have many similarities, and so understanding the embryonic development of this fish can also help with the understanding of human development. Developmental genes in humans have similar functions to those in the zebra fish.

Drugs, pigs and spider goats

The drugs that are used to treat some diseases are simply human **proteins**. It is very expensive to obtain these proteins from other humans, and many of them cannot be produced properly by bacteria. For this reason, transgenic animals, which can produce complex human proteins in their milk at relatively little cost, are beginning to be used. Transgenic goats have been developed to produce a protein that prevents blood clotting, for example. Other transgenic goats have been given spider genes and now produce *biofilaments*, materials that are as strong as steel, in their milk.

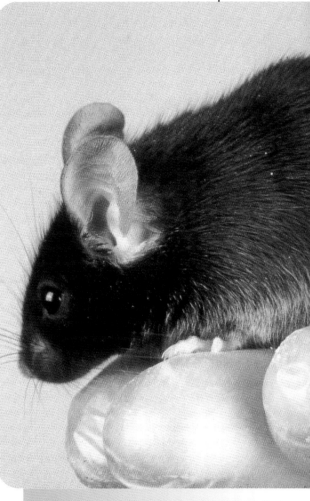

There are many other examples of transgenic animals that could be of benefit to humans. Transgenic pigs grow faster and apparently give a better quality of meat. These pigs are also more resistant to disease. Transgenic sheep have been developed that grow better wool. However, with all these transgenic animals there are safety concerns. Take the example of transgenic salmon, which have been developed with a gene that increases their growth rate. Farming transgenic salmon commercially would produce bigger fish more quickly. However, there are concerns about the possible effects if transgenic salmon were to escape and breed with wild salmon.

This transgenic mouse is used to study the disease muscular dystrophy. Researchers hope to find the genetic causes of this muscle-wasting disease and to develop a therapy to prevent it.

6 Gene therapy

Genetic engineering research has now reached the stage where it is possible to alter a person's **genes**. Defects in single genes are the cause of over 3000 human diseases. **Gene therapy** is a way of treating, curing, or ultimately preventing diseases that result from faulty genes, either by changing the faulty genes or preventing them from being expressed. At present gene therapy is still at the experimental stage.

If a gene is faulty, then the **protein** it codes for will either be faulty or will not be produced. One way of dealing with a genetic illness is to provide the patient with a supply of the gene product (the protein) that is lacking. The protein can be made by bacteria genetically engineered to carry a copy of the properly functioning human gene. Giving protein in this way is called **replacement therapy** and it is already widely used. One example of replacement therapy is in people who are born with a faulty gene for a protein called growth hormone. As its name suggests, growth hormone promotes growth. Children with this faulty gene do not grow properly, and without replacement therapy they would be very short as adults. Replacement therapy works well in this instance, because growth hormone affects many sites throughout the body. However, the growth hormone has to be given by injection over a long period. In other genetic diseases replacement therapy is of limited value, because of the difficulty of targeting the specific cells affected by the illness.

These viruses have been genetically modified to contain the CFTR gene. A faulty CFTR gene is responsible for the disease cystic fibrosis. Researchers aim to use the viruses to give cystic fibrosis patients the 'correct' CFTR gene. Magnification approx. x 250,000.

Somatic and germ-line therapies

Gene therapy is a much more direct approach to dealing with genetic illnesses. Rather than replacing the protein product, gene therapy attempts to replace the faulty gene. It can be targeted either on **somatic** (body) cells, or on germ cells (**gametes**). In somatic gene therapy the patient's **DNA** is altered, but not in such a way that the change is passed on to the next generation. In germ-line gene therapy, egg and sperm cells are changed, with the aim of passing on the changes to the offspring. Germ-line gene therapy is controversial because it would mean allowing new genes to enter the human gene pool.

Many problems stand in the way of successful gene therapy techniques being developed. One of these is finding a reliable way of getting the replacement gene into the body's cells. Currently, the most common means of doing so is to use **viruses**. Viruses, as we have seen, can be engineered to deliver packages of genes into cells. Viruses are an effective way of adding genes into cells, but there can be problems because the body's **immune system** may still recognize the viruses as invaders. This triggers inflammation and other disease responses.

Researchers are also experimenting with other approaches. One is to introduce an artificial **chromosome** into the body's cells. It would take its place alongside the normal chromosomes and would not interfere with them or cause any **mutations**. It would be capable of carrying substantial amounts of **genetic code**, and would not be attacked by the immune system.

Trials in humans

Another problem is in knowing what specific genes do. There are some 30, 000 genes in the human genome and scientists know the function of only a few. Genes may have more than one function if they work together with other genes and some genetic illnesses are caused by more than one gene. There is also the difficulty of targeting specific cells and the danger that the inserted gene will disrupt the expression of a normally functioning gene. Attempting gene therapy without knowing how everything works could lead to unforseen complications.

Most diseases involve the interaction of several genes and the environment. Many people who develop cancer have inherited the disease gene for the disorder, but they may also have contributed to the onset of the disease because of diet, smoking and other environmental factors.

This child was one of the first patients to receive gene therapy (at Necker Children's Hospital, Paris). His immune system did not work properly due to a faulty gene. Scientists introduced genetically engineered white blood cells into his body to correct this potentially fatal condition.

Stem cells

Stem cells are **undifferentiated** cells that can divide indefinitely and can give rise to more specialized tissue cells. A fertilized human egg cell is a type of stem cell that is described as being **totipotent**, meaning that its potential is total – it has the potential to form an entire **organism**. In the first hours after fertilization, this cell divides into two identical totipotent cells. About four days after fertilization and after several more cell divisions, these totipotent cells begin to specialize. They form a hollow sphere of cells called a **blastocyst**.

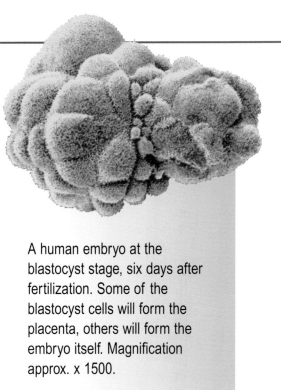

A human embryo at the blastocyst stage, six days after fertilization. Some of the blastocyst cells will form the placenta, others will form the embryo itself. Magnification approx. x 1500.

The outer layer of the blastocyst goes on to form the **placenta**, which nourishes the **embryo** in the **uterus**. The inner layer of the blastocyst goes on to form the many different tissues of the embryo. Although the cells in the inner layer of the blastocyst can form the embryo, they cannot give rise to the placenta. These cells are now said to be **pluripotent** – they can give rise to many, but not all types of cell.

The pluripotent stem cells become more specialized and give rise to cells that have a particular function. Blood stem cells develop into red blood cells, white blood cells and platelets (disc-shaped cell fragments that are important for blood clotting), for example. These more specialized stem cells are called **multipotent**.

Multipotent stem cells are found in the body throughout life. Their job is to replace cells lost through natural wear and tear. For example, blood stem cells are found in the bone marrow and in very small numbers in the bloodstream. Their job is to produce new red blood cells, white blood cells, and platelets to replace cells lost through wear and tear.

Using stem cells

There are a great many ways in which stem cells could be used. One exciting possibility is that embryonic stem cells could be used as 'universal human donor cells', able to provide new liver cells, heart cells, or nerve cells to replace tissues that have been lost or damaged. It may also be possible to treat diseases such as **diabetes**, **Parkinson's disease**, and **Alzheimer's disease**.

Embryonic stem cells could also be used to provide a source of normal human cells of virtually any tissue type for use in drug screening. Embryonic stem cells seem to be 'immortal' when grown in the laboratory – they go on dividing again and again, without aging.

Obtaining stem cells

Stem cell research faces a major problem, because currently the only source of pluripotent human cells is a human embryo. During fertility treatments on women who have problems having children, fertility clinics routinely fertilize more than one egg cell. This means that thousands of unwanted embryos are stored in clinic freezers. Such embryos can be used to produce cultures of stem cells. Obtaining cells in this way is highly controversial. Many people have problems with what they see as the destruction of potential human life.

Until recently it was thought that multipotent stem cells from adult tissue could produce only a limited number of cell types – blood stem cells, for instance, could produce only blood cells. However, experiments with mice suggest that neural (nerve) stem cells may be able to produce a variety of blood cell types if they are placed in the bone marrow. In addition, studies with rats suggest that stem cells found in the bone marrow are able to produce liver cells. If multipotent cells can be persuaded to produce a wider range of cell types, it will be possible to use adult stem cells for cell therapies and perhaps avoid the need to use stem cells from human embryos.

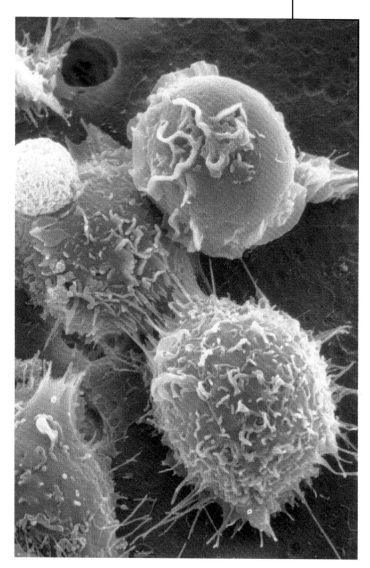

These cells are blood stem cells from human bone marrow. Magnification approx. x 6800.

Making clones

Clones are a group of organisms that are genetically identical. There are many such organisms in nature that result from asexual reproduction, in which a new organism develops from only one parent. Strawberries and other plants that grow from runners are genetically identical to the parent plant, for example. Gardeners often use such techniques as cutting and grafting to produce clones of plants. All the offspring of a single parent are clones. Identical twins are also clones: both twins develop from the same fertilized egg.

Identical twins are natural clones. Identical twins are formed if a fertilized egg cell splits in two, and both cells grow and develop separately.

The clone arrangers

In July 1996, a team of Scottish scientists produced the first live birth of a healthy sheep cloned from another adult sheep. The team took cells from the udder of one sheep and temporarily starved them for a few days to halt their development. An unfertilized egg was removed from a second sheep, and the nucleus was removed. Next, a nucleus from one of the udder cells was transferred into the unfertilized egg. The egg now had a complete set of genes from the first sheep. The egg was then grown for a while in the laboratory before being implanted into the womb of a third sheep, the surrogate mother. The embryo developed normally, and in February 1997 Dolly the sheep was presented to a wondering world.

Transferring a nucleus works because, somehow, some characteristic of the egg cell's cytoplasm can reactivate all of the genes in adult cells so that they behave like stem cells. Scientists are now trying to find out exactly how the cloning procedure succeeds in reprogramming adult cells so they can act like stem cells. Scientists hope that if they succeed in doing so, they might then be able to make stem cells of any type from adult tissue.

Practical cloning

Other uses of cloning that have been suggested include the mass production of animals engineered to carry human genes for the production of **proteins** for use as drugs. The mass production of animals with genetically modified organs to be used as transplant organs for humans is another possibility, as is the mass production of livestock that have been genetically modified to possess desirable characteristics, such as high milk yield in cows. Cloning could perhaps also be used to save endangered species, although the result would be a genetically very weak population because there would be hardly any genetic diversity.

Send in the clones?

Cloning is by no means a certain affair. Dolly was the only survivor of 29 embryos implanted into surrogate mothers. Some embryos did not survive, while others were born with serious genetic defects. The structure of Dolly's **chromosomes** also suggest that her lifespan might be reduced. Other animals such as cattle and mice have been successfully cloned since Dolly, but researchers have had the same problems with large numbers of cloned embryos dying or being born with genetic problems.

Even though there are still many unanswered questions about cloning, there are people who think that human cloning is possible, and childless parents who would be willing to try cloning as a way of getting a child. However, the majority of scientists working in genetics feel strongly that we need to understand much more about cloning before it is safe to attempt it in humans.

Five genetically engineered sheep clones. These clones were not made by micro-injection, like Dolly. Instead, a normally-fertilized egg was removed from the sheep after only a few divisions. The cells that had formed from the initial egg cell were than separated and placed in surrogate mothers.

7 A genetic map

In 1990, a massive international research programme called the Human Genome Project set out to identify all of the approximately 30,000 **genes** in human **DNA** – the human **genome** – and to determine the sequence of the 3 billion or so base pairs that make up human DNA. A working draft covering 90 per cent of the genome was completed in 2000, both by the government-sponsored Human Genome Project and by a private company. By the year 2003, they will finish the sequence with an accuracy of greater than 99.99 per cent.

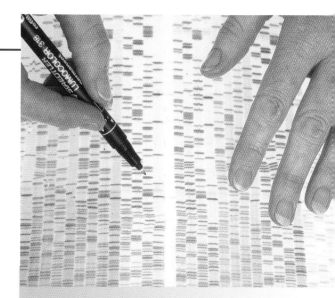

A scientist marking reference points on an X-ray showing DNA sequences. The reference points allow scientists to work out how different sections of the sequence fit together, like pieces of a jigsaw.

As well as mapping human DNA, researchers are also reading the genomes of several other **organisms** including *Escherichia coli*, the fruit fly and the mouse. Even species as seemingly different from us as yeast and fruit flies share many similar genes. Valuable information about human diseases can be gained by studying the role of a similar gene in the fruit fly. For example, the role of some human genes in cancer is understood better than would otherwise have been possible because scientists have studied related genes in flies. In these studies they found that many of these 'cancer' genes are involved in guiding the development of the **embryo**.

The information gained by mapping the genome has been invaluable to geneticists working on genetic illnesses. For example, by1989 geneticists had tracked down only four genes associated with disease by laboriously sorting through inheritance links between sufferers. By 1998, more than 100 genes had been pinpointed. The gene for **cystic fibrosis** was found 1989, after a nine-year hunt. In 1997 the gene for **Parkinson's disease** was identified in just nine days, and precisely described within nine months.

Researchers can electronically scan long stretches of DNA to find genes in the sequence that may be responsible for a particular disease. Those are called **candidate genes**. If a candidate gene actually does play a role in a disease, the sequence of its base pairs should be different in people with the disease. This difference can be minor. Parkinson's disease can result from a change in just a single base pair, which means that just one of the 140 **amino acids** that make up a key **protein** is altered, preventing the protein from doing its job.

Cystic fibrosis

Knowing the DNA sequence of a gene, and therefore the sequence of the amino acids it codes for, sometimes allows researchers to deduce the shape and possibly the function of the protein produced. For instance, when scientists discovered the gene for cystic fibrosis, they recognized it as coding for one of the proteins that are embedded in the membrane of a cell. These proteins act as gateways, allowing certain substances to pass in and out of the cell. It also seemed likely that the protein's task was to allow chloride ions to pass out of the membrane. In cystic fibrosis this protein no longer works properly, which has far-ranging results. Digestive **enzymes** clog a duct between the pancreas and the small intestine, and food can no longer be digested properly. Thick mucus builds up in the respiratory tract, which can cause repeated lung infections. Cysts (sac-like swellings) form in the pancreas, and it becomes fibrous in appearance (hence the name of the disease). Cystic fibrosis is the most common genetic illness affecting Caucasians (white people), and is always fatal.

Although no cure has yet been found for cystic fibrosis, finding the cystic fibrosis gene has been a great advance. Scientists are now investigating the use of **gene therapy** to introduce healthy copies of the gene into the cells of patients with the illness.

Knowing the complete sequence of the human genome will be a remarkable achievement, but it is only a first step. The next step in genome research will be understanding what the function of each gene is, and how the proteins they code work.

A laboratory worker loads DNA samples into a machine which automatically processes the samples and determines their DNA sequences. A huge amount of computing power is needed to store the thousands of different DNA sequences and to find patterns that make it possible to fit them together.

Genome challenges

The first phase of the ambitious international Human Genome Project is nearly complete. Some three dozen other **organisms** (mostly single-celled microbes) have already had their **DNA** completely sequenced. How much can we expect our knowledge of the **genes** that make us human to change our lives, if at all? One certain result will be a much greater understanding of biology. Genetic knowledge is already proving useful in developing more effective treatments for many diseases. For instance the fruit fly, one of the latest organisms to be sequenced, is being used to investigate human disorders such as **Parkinson's disease**.

In the future, a doctor or hospital treating a patient will have the enormous advantage of detailed information about their genetic make-up.

Pharmacogenomics

Pharmacogenomics is the science of using genetic information to predict the safety and effectiveness of a drug. A person's medical records may in the future include the complete base sequence of their **genome** and a catalogue of their genes. It will be possible to use this genetic information to predict how that person will respond to certain drugs, and to other substances such as pollutants in the environment. What this means is that it will be possible to treat each person as a unique genetic individual. Medical treatments will be more specifically tailored to the individual and so will have a greater chance of success. In addition, each person will know their genetic weaknesses. This will give them the chance to change their lifestyle to avoid developing illnesses, for instance heart disease or allergies to certain foodstuffs.

A great many people die every year from bad reactions to drugs, and millions more suffer uncomfortable side-effects. As genes that influence drug response are identified, the number of these bad reactions should be greatly reduced. Drug treatments often fail because the patient lacks the gene that allows the body to use the drug effectively. Knowing in advance whether or not this will happen would give doctors and patients the ability to avoid wasting time and money on ineffective treatments and go straight to the drug with the best chance of working.

Life, but not as we know it?

There are also some worrying consequences of knowing more about individual genetic differences. It is not too hard to imagine a society in which the DNA of every child born is mapped and stored on a vast computer database. It is already possible to use a process called DNA fingerprinting to tell with almost complete certainty whether two samples of DNA are from the same person. Police use this technique to check whether small amounts of DNA (for instance from a person's skin) found at a crime scene match the DNA of a suspect. If everyone's DNA sequence was already held on a computer database, it would be easier to match the DNA from a crime scene to a name on the database. However, many people would feel strongly that holding such information on them would be a restriction to their personal freedom.

DNA 'fingerprints' being compared. These fingerprints are from two parents and their child. Technicians identify sequences common to the mother and child (red) and the father and child (blue). DNA fingerprints can prove conclusively whether or not people are related.

There is also the possibility that people's genetic information would be made available to insurance companies or employers. Insurance companies might charge more to insure people who are more likely to get particular diseases. They could do this even though the person wasn't ill at the time. Employers might even avoid hiring people who could possibly fall seriously ill in the future.

Genetic engineers already have the knowledge to create synthetic genes by splicing together DNA nucleotides. As our knowledge of genes and development increases, it may become possible for scientists to create from scratch, in the laboratory, a fully functioning living cell. This might seem like an exciting prospect, but it also raises serious worries. Do we really know enough about living things and how they work to be sure about creating what would effectively be a new form of life?

Genetic engineering can have immense benefits, but it can also cause serious problems. The more that we understand about the uses and the limitations of genetic engineering, the better we will be at making the difficult decisions about what kinds of genetic engineering we would like to see, and what is not acceptable.

Some major events in genetics

1856	Austrian monk and botanist Gregor Mendel starts his breeding experiments on peas (that will lead him to state the laws of heredity)
1858	English naturalists Charles Darwin and Alfred Russel Wallace announce the theory of Natural Selection: individuals that are better adapted to their environment survive, reproduce and pass on their characteristics
1859	Darwin publishes *The Origin of Species*
1866	Mendel publishes the results of his investigations on inheritance in pea plants
1871	Nitrogen and phosphorous material discovered in cell nuclei, now known as the genetic material DNA
1873	First accurate description of mitosis
1900	Mendel's principles were independently discovered by several scientists, and verified, marking the beginning of modern genetics
1902	Chromosomes identified as carriers of genes when cell division is shown to be connected with heredity
1920s	Major component of chromosomes is shown to be DNA
1944	Role of DNA in genetic inheritance is first demonstrated by US biologist Oswald Avery
1953	US biologist James Watson and English molecular biologist Francis Crick announce the three-dimensional structure of the DNA molecule as a double helix. They also propose a mechanism for replication of DNA.
1954	US cosmologist George Gamow suggests that the 'genetic code' consists of the order of triplets of bases in the DNA molecule
1956	Humans shown to have 23 pairs of chromosomes
1958	US geneticists show that genes act by regulating definite chemical events in the cell
1966	Genetic code 'cracked', as it is shown that DNA has triplet codons that specify each of the twenty amino acids.
1969	US geneticists isolate a single gene for the first time
1973	Technique of recombinant DNA developed by US scientists. This marks the beginning of genetic engineering.
1981	Insulin made by bacteria is the first genetically engineered product to go on sale
1984	Genetic fingerprinting technique of identifying individuals (as DNA pattern is unique to each person) developed by British geneticist Alec Jeffreys
1988	Human Genome Project begun, with the goal of determining the entire sequence of bases in human DNA
1990	First successful gene therapy carried out in USA for a girl with SCID – a rare immunodeficiency disease caused by a genetic defect
1993	'Flavr Savr' tomatoes, the first genetically engineered food (for longer shelf-life), are marketed
1997	Scottish geneticists at the Roslin Institute clone a sheep (called Dolly)
1999	Complete base sequence of human chromosome 22 announced: there are over 500 genes
2000	Human Genome Project presents its preliminary results: each of the body's 100 trillion cells contains some 3.1 billion base units – only one per cent of these are thought to be transcribed. We may have as few as 30,000 genes!

Glossary

agar gel a jelly-like substance made from seaweed, which is used as a growth medium for bacteria

AIDS (acquired immune deficiency syndrome) a viral disease that seriously damages a person's immune system

Alzheimer's disease a disease that causes memory loss, poor mental ability, and eventually physical problems

amino acid a naturally occurring chemical used by cells to make proteins

antibiotics chemicals that destroy or stop the growth of disease-causing bacteria

asexual reproduction reproduction in which an organism produces genetically identical copies (clones) of itself

bacteriophage (phage) a virus that infects bacteria

base a type of chemical found in genetic material. There are four different bases in DNA.

blastocyst a hollow, fluid-filled ball of cells, an early stage in the growth of a fertilized human egg

callus a growth of unspecialized cells that forms in a plant over a wound

candidate gene a gene that has been identified as perhaps being the site of a particular genetic disease

catalyst a substance that speeds up a chemical reaction – enzymes are the catalysts of biological reactions.

chromosome a DNA molecule coiled around protein molecules called histones. Chromosones are present in the nuclei of eukaroyte cells. During nuclear division, they become visible as rod-like structures.

clones organisms that are genetically identical to each other

codon a sequence of three bases on RNA molecules that together code for a particular amino acid

cotyledons structures in a plant seed that become the plant's first leaves, or act as a food store

cystic fibrosis a disease caused by a faulty gene that involves large amount of mucus production, especially in the lungs, leading to repeated lung infections

cytoplasm all the contents of a cell outside the nucleus

deoxyribonucleic acid see DNA

diabetes a disease caused by a lack of the hormone insulin, in which there is no control over the levels sugar in the blood

dicot (*dicotyledon*) a type of plant that has two cotyledons or seed leaves. Roses, dandelions, and violets are common dicots.

DNA (deoxyribonucleic acid) the genetic material of living things. DNA carries instructions for constructing, maintaining and reproducing living cells.

DNA polymerase the enzyme that is involved in replicating one strand of DNA from another

embryo a very young organism in the early stages of development, before it emerges from the egg or seed, or is born from its mother's uterus

enzyme a type of protein that controls one of the thousands of chemical reactions inside a living cell

eukaryote one of the two basic types of cell. All kinds of living things except bacteria are made up of eukaryote cells.

exons stretches of DNA that do code for a protein

gall a swelling produced on a plant caused by the attack of a parasite. Crown galls are caused by the bacterium *Agrobacterium tumefaciens*.

gametes the sex cells in organisms that reproduce sexually. During sexual reproduction a male and a female gamete fuse, or join, to form a new organism.

gene a stretch of DNA that contains the information to make all or part of a protein

gene expression the production of a protein from a gene or genes. When a gene is expressed it gives rise to characteristics in the organism, such as pink flowers in a pea plant, or curly hair in a child.

gene probe a short stretch of DNA whose sequence of bases matches up with a unique part of a particular gene. The probe is 'tagged' with radioactivity, and can be used to find a particular gene.

gene splicing the process of cutting open a DNA molecule, inserting a new gene or genes, and then closing it up again

gene therapy treatment for a genetic disease that aims to replace a faulty gene with a properly working one

genetic code the way in which the four bases that make up DNA or RNA chains code for the twenty amino acids that make up proteins. Each set of three bases codes for one amino acid or a stop condon.

genome the complete set of genetic information of a particular individual

histones proteins in the cell nucleus that are closely associated with DNA

immune system the system that protects an organism from infection and disease

immunize to protect a person against a particular illness by stimulating their immune system

introns the sections of a gene in a eukaryote cell that do not code for a protein or part of a protein

Glossary

lactose a complex sugar made of galactose and glucose

messenger RNA the molecule that carries the genetic code for a protein out of the nucleus to the ribosomes, where protein assembly takes place

micro-injection the use of an ultra-fine needle to inject DNA into a cell

micro-organisms single-celled organisms that are too small to be seen with the naked eye

monocot a type of plant that has one cotyledon or seed leaf. Tulips, grasses and cereals such as wheat are common monocots.

multipotent a cell that is capable of giving rise to a number of different cell types is multipotent

mutation any change in a cell's genes or in a chromosome's structure, or a change in the number of chromosomes in a cell

nucleotides small molecules that join together in chains to form DNA and RNA molecules

nucleus the biggest and most obvious structure inside a eukaryote cell. The nucleus is where the cell's genetic material is stored.

opines substances made by tumour cells in plants

organism any type of living thing

Parkinson's disease a disease of the nervous system in which the muscles become rigid and the patient cannot move

phage see bacteriophage

placenta a structure produced by the fertilized egg in mammals, which connects to the uterus and obtains nutrients for the growing baby from the mother's blood

plasmid a small, circular piece of DNA found in many bacteria. Plasmids often give bacteria resistance to an antibiotic.

pluripotent a cell that is capable of producing all the different cells in a human or mammal, but not the placenta

polypeptide a large number of amino acids joined together to form one long molecule. A protein consists of one or more polypeptides.

prokaryote the simplest type of living cell. Bacteria are prokaryotes; all other living things are made up of eukaryote cells.

promoter a section of DNA immediately before a gene, where the enzyme responsible for producing messenger RNA for that gene attaches

proteins substances that make up many cell parts and control a cell's reactions. Proteins are large molecules made up of many subunits called amino acids.

protoplast a plant cell without its cell wall

radioactive a substance whose atoms gradually break down, emitting some kind of radiation (high-energy waves or subatomic particles)

recombinant DNA DNA from one source containing some material from another source, for instance viral DNA containing a human gene

recombinant virus a virus containing DNA from another source within its own DNA

regulatory proteins proteins that are involved in controlling whether or not a gene is expressed

replacement therapy treatment for a genetic disease in which a protein that is lacking due to a faulty gene is injected into the patient

respiration the process by which living things obtain oxygen from the environment to be used in the breakdown and release of energy from their food

restriction enzymes enzymes that cut DNA molecules at particular points, breaking it up into fragments

reverse transcriptase an enzyme that makes it possible to make a DNA molecule from an RNA template

ribonucleic acid see RNA

ribosomes small structures within cells that are the sites of protein synthesis

RNA (ribonucleic acid) a substance related to DNA which plays an important part in protein synthesis

somatic cell any cell in a multicellular organism that is not a reproductive cell (a gamete)

stem cell an unspecialized cell that can divide to form several or many different cell types

substrate the substance on which an enzyme acts

surrogate mother a female that incubates and gives birth to an embryo that is not her own

Ti plasmid a small, circular piece of DNA found in the bacterium *Agrobacterium tumefaciens* that causes a plant to grow a gall

totipotent a stem cell that is capable of dividing and growing to produce a complete organism

transcription the production of a single-stranded RNA molecule from a section of DNA

transfer RNA a type of RNA that is involved in carrying amino acids to the ribosomes and is involved in attaching them to protein chains

transgenic organism an organism containing a gene or genes from another organism

translation the process by which information coded on messenger RNA is transformed into a protein

undifferentiated a cell that has not become specialized for a particular task

uterus the organ in a female mammal where its offspring develop before birth

vaccine a substance, often dead or inactivated disease-causing micro-organisms, which stimulates the immune system and gives immunity to a disease

virus small section of DNA or RNA surrounded by a protective protein 'coat', which can infect a living cell and cause it to produce copies of itself

Further reading and websites

Books

Advanced Biology: Biology Principles and Applications, C J Clegg, John Murray, 2000
Coordinated Science: Higher Biology, Richard Fosbery and Jean McLean, Heinemann Library, 1996
Improving Nature? The Science and Ethics of Genetic Engineering, Michael J Reiss, Roger Straughan, Cambridge University Press, 2001
Life processes: Cells and Systems, Holly Wallace, Heinemann Library, 2002
Science at the Edge, Cloning, Sally Morgan, Heinemann Library, 2002
Science at the Edge, Genetic Modification of Food, Sally Morgan, Heinemann Library, 2002
Science Fact Files: Genetics, Richard Beatty, Hodder Wayland, 2001

Websites

Cells Alive (http://www.cellsalive.com/)
     A good introduction to the cell, with homework help.
How stuff works – Cells (http://www.howstuffworks.com/cell.htm)
     Worth a visit to discover unusual aspects of life at cell level.
Cells R Us (http://www.icnet.uk/kids/cellsrus/cellsrus.html)
     Animated cell division.
Cell biology tutorial (http://www.biology.arizona.edu/cell_bio/cell_bio.html)
     Revision on the structure and function of the cell.
Natural history of genes (http://gslc.genetics.utah.edu/)
     Challenge nature and build your own DNA molecule.
Frank Potter's Science gems (http://sciencegems.com/life.html)
     A wealth of references all about cells.
Slouching towards creation (http://www.pathfinder.com/TIME/cloning/home.html)
     Scientific breakthroughs in cloning.
I can do that! (http://www.eurekascience.com/ICanDoThat/index.htm)
     Cells, DNA and all that brought to life.
Dolly at the Roslin Institute (http://www.roslin.ac.uk)
     Background information on cloning and genetic engineering.

Index